ABSINTHE & IRON CAGES

ALSO BY WALSH WETTENGLE

FICTION

Snowman (Coming June 2025)

Absinthe & Iron Cages

Words by
Walsh Wettengle

Including:

Smoke
August 23, 1726 (i)
August 23, 1726 (ii)
It Happened
Toulouse-Lautrec Poster
Deprived
Myoclonic Twitch
vertigo
from Dr. Reginald's Private Journal: 11-27-94
nepentheboy
Winchester Goose - a silly sestina

Copyright © 1994, 2025 by Walsh Wettengle

All rights reserved. No part of this publication may be reproduced, distributed, or transmitted in any form or by any means, including photocopying, recording, or other electronic or mechanical methods, without the prior written permission of the publisher, except in the case of brief quotations embodied in critical reviews and certain other noncommercial uses permitted by copyright law.

Published by: Walsh Wettengle
Seattle, WA
First Edition
ISBN: 979-8-9986810-0-4
Cover Art created using ChatGPT

smoke

Beauty smokes cancer diamonds,
coveted by her festering king.
as her sister Dear stumbles in
the cemetery, bleats like a choir
and farts blood and vodka.
An angel clutches the tramp
and floods her house of cards
with bile, absinthe, and iron cages.
The ribbon crucifies the castle of
prophets with a rusted razor blade.
Heaven. Brothel where boys vibrate
in the rain like ombrophobes, bronzed
until the box of puddles drowns the altar.
Bells belch ash onto strangled doorsteps
howling chickens and crossing themselves.
We hope it goes no further...

undated

Toulouse-Lautrec Poster

A pair of oversized pink souffles,
erupt from her cranium, hover
over carefully painted face.
Black outline of her hair is fire
in a torrent of chow mein noodles
An entry wound adorns her
bloody rose chest and her
eyes, vacant, long
after her soul has fled.
She is no woman again
but a gaudy trollop arrested
with her wrists restrained at her back.
Bends gender again and
laughs at their faces after.
Look pretty for the
morgue, babe, and clench
your teeth as he rides you.
Dress hiked up a hundred
times like a wet peacock.
Jealousy's face and a gun
slam dancing into her
chipped nails and the cut,
where she tore the lid to the
saran wrap box.
Serrated edges and
                    hot wax
                            dripping
                                    into the
                                            cornflakes.

Feb 7 1994

vertigo

dart away
you dare to not meet my eyes
around us
dancers drive like pistons
steaming
sweat, spit, angst, they secrete
sweetly
as they thirst to bleed
not hard
to spot you in the thrall
black hair,
a shock of plaster-white face
sidelong.
shows me the smear my lips made
still taste
make-up, the memory comes
fumbling
drunken hands and lips
lingering
too long on artificial pale
dizzy
strobes cover my misstep
fucking
clumsy
frantic drones writhe like an
ocean,
around us, surround us, a boy
ravenous
cuts between us, hard, shirtless,
pierced naval
I know this one and I mouth
"later"
he takes it away, a vow,
seize the dance.

Oct 9 1994

from Dr. Reginald's Private Journal: 11-27-94.

Three times a month we share
this space, these antiseptic walls
colored to calm, you or me?
The walls between us are
colored invisible but I touch them.
Secrets pass from your eyes that
will never part your lips.
I conquer your dark to
make my light, like a mantis
devouring its mate, I make
your thoughts my own.
Reversed, I become your
patient without a whisper
from your hurt. Your hand covers
mine to pass the fire from me to me.
Walls are blasted, mouths collide,
tongues explore where therapy
can never take us. Bodies open
in place of minds.

Nov 27 1994

Winchester Goose
--a silly sestina--

After eating, I bitch and force
him to retreat outside to smoke.
It does something to his face.
Makes it ugly. "David
always squints his eyes when he drags,"
I think, gripping my typewriter.

I have an old typewriter.
Ancient so I have to force
the keys back down when they drag.
Ink on my fingers. "Come smoke
with me." "Leave me alone, David."
Black smudges of ink on my face.

A scholar, I study faces,
each as different as a typewriter,
my excuse to ignore David
while he speaks, while he forces
conversation until a smoking
argument erupts. I drag

myself outside to suck a drag
from his cigarette, scrunch my face,
and puke the acrid smoke.
I want to crawl into my typewriter
because he won. For his attention I force
feed his ego. I can only stand David

because he really knows how to fuck. David,
I can't think without my dick so drag
me back to the bed, the fire, and force
the fear out of my face,
out of my typewriter.
He brags about fucking: "I smoked

him," he laughs. He smokes
whenever we fight. David's

smile makes me want to sell my typewriter
sometimes, and sometimes I want to drag
it in slow motion across his face
and feel his nicotine-stained teeth split from the
force.

After the smoke clears, I don't need to be dragged
into David's arms, his hypnotic eyes, his face.
I've forgotten the typewriter, replaced it with
another force.

Apr 18 1994

nepentheboy

Lips touched for the last time.
Like a snapped branch
he broke the embrace.
You're sick of kissing chapped lips anyway.
Rain black as the wind smashed your sigh
so you cry behind your hand like a child.
Smile, like he doesn't talk to you and
smell the copper syrup, estrangement
that won't scrub away. It scorched
the last kiss he gave you, roughness
of chest behind suave veneer
stirred you like a machine as his
stiff shadow fell across your face,
sharper than cut glass and colder.
His parting laugh. You said:
"Don't laugh. Far away monkeys laugh.
Far away spittle dries on
their matted chins and their
spasmodic bodies twitch,
electrocuted by your words."
Every stinging word that
he called harmony... harmony...
Then riot is harmony.
Disease is bliss.
I bled when he spoke.
Like you, I soundlessly
screamed at his touch.

Apr 1994 - Nov 1996

August 23, 1726 (l)

A thousand gaslit lamps entertain one
dead man whose electric touch grasps many
hearts at once. A wet mist cloaks around him
and carries him along like a million
dew fairies intent on imbibing
a brew of milk and blood as thick as
the shell that carries it. Enslaved to his
blatant lust, he cries mutely into the
night, parting the fog and waking
children wet with piss. Shaken with horrid
visions, you roll away from your
love, lips still wet with kiss and more, but
dread thickens faster than semen when your
name is shrieked voicelessly through darkened
streets.
As you wipe condensation from glass
and peer without, no stars except two
stare back, past you at sleeping lover.
A reflection it ceases to be
when it shatters like a burst
of tiny, silver touches. Did your heart
stop then or when you saw the
face of the thing that killed you?

Undated

August 23, 1726 (ll)

It was 1:30 am that tuesday when
he pulled you into the night, into
a world you'd never seen. Blood turned black
as wet stringy fingers of your hair
he touched to his lips, an insane kiss.
His face, as familiar as the rain that
began to drip into the smothered
blanket of fog embracing you as one.
You remember his requiem as vague
as the love spent moments ago in your
room where He picks through mirrored triangles
of bloody glass, the only signs of you.
An exhilaration of pumping blood
gushing like a hot spring every night when
you feed. A thrill never to be taken
harshly or unclean, or without seeing
his face again, a recurring nightmare
as sensual as a tainted caress
or a promise as savage as your mouth
descending on a puddle of rancid
liquor. Can you still taste it?

Undated

It happened

I said to Charles, "I don't
think you should've driven away
after you hit that woman."
He shifted, uncomfortable, as did
i after it happened, when
out of the night a small woman
stepped into impact and shifted
into roadside ditch.
She walked limplessly away,
but things happen inside people.
They live on when smashed.
Insides are pulp and bones
are jelly. When they open
their mouths to speak only
blood erupts and I can't
speak that language.

Nov 27 1994

Myoclonic Twitch

Spiral darkness
drips into my mind
like drops of molten lead
scars my thoughts
paints pictures of
kingdoms, hells,
cities of silver and molasses.
A caravan of horses
thunders hooflessly past
leaving bloody
stump-prints across my chest.
Trampled, I clutch at
the dream beside me.
He smiles and spits me
into the snow where I am
lowered by a dumbwaiter
onto a heap of kangaroos.
A sightless infant,
I grope hungrily on
a body I can't see
which begins to warmly melt.
I touch some to my tongue
and taste the Earth.
Spinning as fast as a stolen throat
I am restrained by Lethargy,
kite-strings, and fleshless hands.
Inside a tragic world where Bosch
meets Demuth and giant soup spoons
fly around my head proclaiming
Mo Gaffney as queen.
Breath escapes into the vacuum of
soiled footwear on a bus where
everyone expects me to snap my fingers
like a torch and disappear into
a crowd of sweaty nuns smoking
clove cigarettes and dancing
under pulsing blacklights.
Nudging past an undulating street

queen with hair finer than mine I
open a whim where Neil and Tori
hold thorny branches. They flog
a bloated fish man whose clammy
wet saturates my sheets where I jerk
awake in my own sweat remembering
the smell of the fish man and
the ivory skin of the dream king.

                                                Feb 27 1994

Deprived

I feel magical when
it snows at night.
The world becomes
a still, white landscape,
a quiet romance.
It doesn't snow where
you are: the land of
smog and honey.
I smile and am
 truly elated that
there is one more
small pleasure you
are denied.

                                                    Dec 4 1994

www.ingramcontent.com/pod-product-compliance
Lightning Source LLC
LaVergne TN
LVHW050734250326
834741LV00031B/197/J